Masterclass Karate

Masterclass Karate
Kicking Techniques
(Keri Waza)

Michael Robert Berger

P.O. Box 491788, Los Angeles, CA 90049

www.empirebooks.net

Disclaimer

Please note that the author and publisher of this book are NOT RESPONSIBLE in any manner whatsoever for any injury that may result from practicing the techniques and/or following the instructions given within. Since the physical activities described herein may be too strenuous in nature for some readers to engage in safely, it is essential that a physician be consulted prior to training.

First published in 2007 by Empire Books
Copyright © 2007 by Empire Books

All rights reserved. No part of this publication may be reproduced or utilized in any form or by any means, electronic or mechanical, including photocopying, recording, or by any information storage and retrieval system, without prior written permission from Empire Books.

First edition
06 05 04 03 02 01 00 99 98 97 1 3 5 7 9 10 8 6 4 2

Printed in the United States of America.

Empire Books
P.O. Box 491788
Los Angeles, CA 90049
www.empirebooks.net

ISBN-13: 978-1-933901-27-5
ISBN-10: 1-933901-27-6

Library of Congress Cataloging-in-Publication Data

Berger, Michael, 1958-
  Masterclass karate : kicking techniques / by Michael Berger. -- 1st ed.
    p. cm.
  Includes index.
  ISBN 1-933901-27-6 (pbk. : alk. paper)
  1. Karate--Training. 2. Karate--Kicking. I. Title.
  GV1114.3.B47 2006
  796.815'3--dc22
            2006024345

About the Cover Art

In the Japanese calligraphy and associated brushed art on the cover and throughout the book, renowned Shodo Master Hirokazu Kosaka expresses his unique interpretation of the subject matter.

Kosaka-san's rendition of the *enso*, or Zen Circle, combined with the attached stick symbolizing the traditional walking staff, (further symbolic of the leg) is indeed unique and representative of the concept of kicking utilized in karate.

The enso has profound significance to Zen Buddhists, and is most often thought of to represent the void, truth, enlightenment, absolute, no beginning/no end of all phenomena.

In Zen Buddhism and ancient Chinese, Daoist, East Indian, and Tibetan history, the staff is mentioned often, and is associated with such notable figures as Bodhidharma, Hakuin, Wumen, Baqiao, Wuzhou, and Milarepa. It has been represented as having the power to pass universal or transcendent knowledge to others, symbolic of the flexible nature of the pure essence of "original mind," and as a walking staff to cross rivers and climb to new heights(perhaps both figuratively and metaphorically). It is associated further with faith, devotion, discipline, strength, and unmistaken practice. Additionally, it represents the link between Zen and the martial arts.

In his unique depiction of the staff in combination with the enso, Mr. Kosaka relates the staff to the leg used in kicking, supporting the enlightened mind.

About the Author

MICHAEL ROBERT BERGER began his journey into *"the way"* as a young amateur athlete whose interests, in addition to martial arts, included boxing, wrestling, and other sports, as well as meditation and academics. In 1983, following a successful career as a scholarship athlete (wrestling), he graduated from the University of Utah with a B.A. in English and relocated to Japan to further his martial arts training, which he had begun with the Japan Karate Association. He would reside there for a cumulative time period of over four years spanning a ten year period.

After enduring several hours a day of arduous training at a small country dojo in rural Japan, he was awarded his Black Belt in 1984 by legendary Chief Instructor Masatoshi Nakayama at the JKA World Headquarters in Tokyo. That same year, he qualified for and competed in the All-Japan Tournament at the Nippon Budokan. In 1986, he would return to compete again in the Budokan as part of an elite International Team. That same year, he became one of few foreigners ever to be accepted to train at Takushoku University, a perennial power renowned for its rigorous karate program and alma mater to many JKA legends.

A successful competitor both nationally and internationally, he holds numerous titles in both kata and kumite, including a 2nd place finish in *kumite* at the IKA World Cup in 2000, and several titles in Japan. He currently teaches in San Pedro, Calif., and continues training and teaching under the tutelage of Soke Takayuki Kubota at the International Karate Association World Headquarters in Los Angeles. He continues to travel, teaching seminars worldwide, and makes frequent trips to Japan and China to further his training. He has been featured in numerous newspaper and magazine articles, and is an actor, writer, poet, musician, and Zen practitioner. He is currently pursuing an advanced graduate degree in Traditional Oriental Medicine. For more details, please visit *www.wayoflifekarate.com*.

Acknowledgements

Thanking all of the people responsible for making this book happen would indeed be an impossible task. Throughout my life, I have had the good fortunate to have been touched by so many people. I am sure that many of you have no idea of the profound and lasting effect you have had upon my life. For me, karate is not something that I do… it is something that I am. I am so grateful for having been placed and guided along this path. It has led me to great friendship, understanding, compassion, and realization. I owe everything to karate. After over 30 years of training, I am still learning and still being so profoundly touched by the teachings, the lessons, and the people. In one way or another, karate is directly or indirectly responsible for everything that I am…I have many *zenga,* Japanese brushed calligraphy Zen sayings in my home and in my dojo. Some of my favorites say, "To a man of satori, nothing happens," "Each moment, only once," and "Fearlessness." Through karate-do, perhaps we can get a glimpse of deeper understanding that empowers us and gives us strength and freedom. Perhaps we can see the oneness of life, and experience the true compassion that follows. Perhaps we can discover who we really are…and become truly free, and experience no fear. All of these are attainable gifts that can be redeemed through the study of karate-do, the bridge to Zen.
Although it would be impossible to thank everyone here, it would not be appropriate if I did not express my deepest gratitude to those of whom I could not have done this without …

First, **to my parents and my family**, for their unconditional love and unending support and encouragement, in spite of me taking, *"the road less traveled by."* Without the unselfish support of my family, none of this could have been possible.

Secondly, **to all of my teachers**, for their great patience and unselfish sharing. I probably learned more about life from all of you than I did karate.

I would like to specifically acknowledge the following whose contributions were particularly memorable:

Sensei Teruo Honda of TDK Karate Club in Chiba Prefecture, my first teacher in Japan, who spent countless hours teaching me privately every day on an old tatami mat at a factory in rural Japan, and never accepted a single yen. Sensei Honda remains a great friend to this day.

Sensei Noriaki Watanabe, my sempai at the Shotojuku Dojo in Narashino, Chiba Prefecture, for treating me like a family member, teaching me the significance of real fighting spirit, and introducing me to both **Yoshioka Sensei** (Chuo University), and **Shoji Sensei**, to both of whom I wish to express my deepest gratitude. Nabe Sempai has the spirit of a tiger and a kind, humble heart. He helped me in so many ways, and continues to be a dear friend.

Sensei Hiroshi Shoji, who so kindly invited me as the first *gaijin-san* into his humble home in Saitama Prefecture. Shoji Sensei taught me great lessons of real *budo*. I had the privilege of visiting his home again just months before his passing, and will always remember his bright, cheerful eyes and contagious laugh. I also thank him for the gift of allowing me to have his name on my belt.

Sensei Masatoshi Nakayama, whose presence and indomitable spirit, combined with his generosity and strength, has always made a lasting impression on me. His passion about karate was unrivaled, and those of us who trained with him are keeping that spirit alive, thanks to my good friend Jon Keeling, with the Hoitusugan Seminars, named in honor of Nakayama Sensei's personal dojo near Ebisu Station. Most of all, I am eternally indebted to Nakayama Sensei for stressing to me the importance of Zen practice, and for sharing with me the phrase *Ken Zen Ichi*, which since then became the name of my dojo organization *(Ken Zen Ichi Kan).*

Sensei Tsuyama and the members of Takushoku University Karate Team. A special thanks to **Naka Sempai,** the captain while I was there, who took it easy on me and saved me from being slaughtered by the others during the brutal training there …**Naka Sensei** went on to become JKA All-Japan and World Champion, and is now one of the most famous teachers in Japan. He remains a great friend and continues to welcome me with his big smile and positive attitude whenever I am in Japan. *"Every day, Happy day."*

Sensei Ohishi and the members of the Komazawa University Karate Team, for allowing me to train with them often during my stay in Japan.

Zen Master Dennis Genpo Merzel Roshi, head of the White Plum Asanga and Kanzeon Sangha International, Founder of the Big Mind Process, for giving me a tiny glimpse of *"Big Mind"* through his teachings. I am deeply indebted to him for his guidance, inspiration and patience with me as a humble student, and for deepening my belief in Zen as the ultimate practice.

Mr. Tino T. Khvang, my dear friend and training partner, for kindly consenting to help by being my partner in the photos for this book. I appreciate your unselfish friendship.

Mr. Hirokazu Kosaka, shodo master, Kyudo no Sensei, and curator at the Japanese American Cultural and Community Center in Los Angeles, who graciously and generously assisted me by preparing all of the Japanese characters and shodo artwork seen in the book.

A special thanks to my current teacher and friend, **Grandmaster Takayuki Kubota,** founder of Go-Soku Ryu and the International Karate Association… and to the entire IKA family. Soke Kubota graciously accepted me into his dojo over ten years ago, and continues to be a great inspiration in my life. Through his living example, my life and my path have been unequivocally and permanently altered. He is the real *"Last Samurai",* and his passion, courage, knowledge, strength, and unselfish compassion are truly unparalleled. *"Soke! Domo arigato gozaimashita!"*

Lastly, and certainly not least, to the publishers at **Empire Books** for their patience with me, and for making this idea become reality.

CONTENTS

Introduction 15
General Considerations 17

MAE GERI— *"Front Kick"*

Description 21
Common Mistakes 24
Advanced/Alternative Application 26
Training Exercises 27
Offensive Combinations
   Direct Attacks—Attacking directly and decisively 30
   Indirect Attacks—Utilizing feints, set-ups, and invitations 33
Defensive Combinations
   Counterattacks using Maai/Tai Sabaki (Distance/shifting) 38
   Counterattacks using Uke Waza (Blocking techniques) 42

MAWASHI GERI— *"Roundhouse Kick"*

Description 45
Common Mistakes 50
Advanced/Alternative Application 51
Training Exercises 52
Offensive Combinations
   Direct Attacks—Attacking directly and decisively 60
   Indirect Attacks—Utilizing feints, set-ups, and invitations 65
Defensive Combinations
   Counterattacks using Maai/Tai Sabaki (Distance/shifting) 67
   Counterattacks using Uke Waza (Blocking techniques) 72

GYAKU MAWASHI GERI—*"Reverse Roundhouse Kick"*

Description 79
Common Mistakes 82
Training Exercises 83
Offensive Combinations
   Direct Attacks—Attacking directly and decisively 85
   Indirect Attacks—Utilizing feints, set-ups, and invitations 88
Defensive Combinations
   Counterattacks using Maai/Tai Sabaki (Distance/shifting) 92
   Counterattacks using Uke Waza (Blocking techniques) 94

URA MAWASHI GERI—*"Hook Kick"*

Description 97
Common Mistakes 100
Training Exercises 101
Offensive Combinations
   Direct Attacks—Attacking directly and decisively 102
   Indirect Attacks—Utilizing feints, set-ups, and invitations 103
Defensive Combinations
   Counterattacks using Maai/Tai Sabaki (Distance/shifting) 104
   Counterattacks using Uke Waza (Blocking techniques) 106

USHIRO GERI—*"Back Kick"*

Description 113
Common Mistakes 116
Training Exercises 117
Offensive Combinations
   Direct Attacks—Attacking directly and decisively 122
   Indirect Attacks—Utilizing feints, set-ups, and invitations 126
Defensive Combinations
   Counterattacks using Maai/Tai Sabaki (Distance/shifting) 132
   Counterattacks using Uke Waza (Blocking techniques) 136

YOKO GERI KEKOMI— *"Side Thrust Kick"*

Description 139
Common Mistakes 144
Training Exercises 146
Offensive Combinations
   Direct Attacks—Attacking directly and decisively 150
   Indirect Attacks—Utilizing feints, set-ups, and invitations 154
Defensive Combinations
   Counterattacks using Maai/Tai Sabaki (Distance/shifting) 158
   Counterattacks using Uke Waza (Blocking techniques) 160

YOKO GERI KEAGE— *"Side Snap Kick"*

Description 163
Common Mistakes 166
Training Exercises 167
Offensive Combinations
   Direct Attacks—Attacking directly and decisively 168
   Indirect Attacks—Utilizing feints, set-ups, and invitations 172
Defensive Combinations
   Counterattacks using Maai/Tai Sabaki (Distance/shifting) 176
   Counterattacks using Uke Waza (Blocking techniques) 177

LESS FREQUENTLY USED KICKS

MAE GERI KEKOMI— *"Front thrust kick"*
   Description 179
   Application 180

OTOSHI GERI— *"Axe Kick"*
   Description 181
   Application 182

MIKAZUKI GERI—*"Crescent kick"*
    Description 183
    Application 184

MAWASHI UCHI—*"Inside Crescent Kick"*
    Description 185
    Application 186

HIZA GERI—*"Knee Kick"*
    Description 187
    Application 188

TOBI GERI—*"Jumping Kick"*
    Description 189

Conclusion 190

INTRODUCTION

I remember clearly the early part of May, 1984 at the Japan Karate Association's old Hombu (Headquarters) Dojo near Ebisu Station in Tokyo. I had just participated in an early spring morning *dan* testing conducted by Nakayama Sensei. There were over 100 of us who had taken the examination, and now we waited anxiously to hear the comments of our great master.

Nakayama Sensei was a man of great presence and few words…but I will always remember him telling us, "More kicking techniques! You must practice more kicking techniques!"

My subsequent training over the last two and a half decades or so with many of the world's greatest masters has further reinforced and strengthened this belief, yet though I have endeavored assiduously to expand and refine the use of *keri-waza*, I am far from mastering them.

In truth, *keri-waza*, or kicking techniques, comprises about one half of the weaponry of the arsenal in karate. Perhaps of more importance, being that the legs are so tremendously superior in both strength and reach to the arms, neglecting the proper development of kicking can be only result in a partial development of the art, and thus in obvious ultimate defeat.

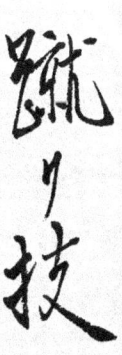

Conversely, proper use of kicking opens up a full array of possibilities in both offensive and defensive maneuvers. One of my teachers used to tell me, "When you want to punch, kick. When you want to kick, punch." One sets up the other, and they become complimentary to each other. When the entire body can be used with equal ease, when the techniques flow fluidly, effortlessly, and spontaneously, without the limitation of conscious thought… only then, do we get a glimpse of understanding the true nature of the original mind, of the budo mind.

Lastly, I would like to offer some words that may serve to balance the analytical nature of the techniques described here. Although I feel it important to have an intellectual understanding of both the mechanics and usage of the various techniques to follow, nothing can replace repetitive practice. Only through continued and repetitive practice is one able to make his/her own discoveries and gain a deeper and lasting insight that transcends words. Best said, in the words of Yamaoka Tesshu, the great 19th century swordsman, calligrapher, poet and Zen Master, *"DAMATTE KEIKO!"* which translates roughly to "SHUT UP AND PRACTICE !"

Best wishes to all of you in your training.

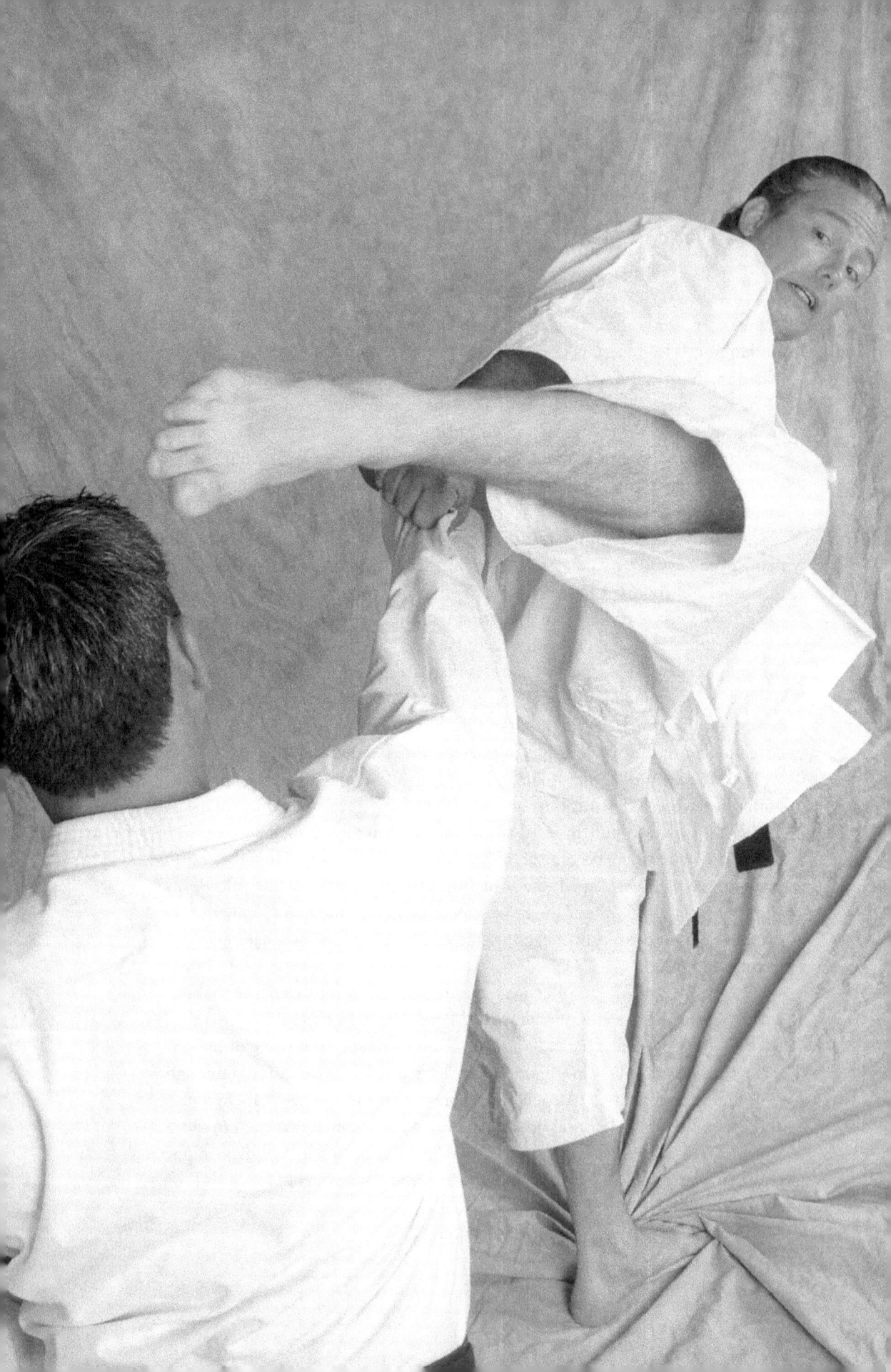

General Considerations

Mastery of Kicking Techniques—General Considerations
Some general principles can be applied universally with regard to the mastery of kicking techniques. Some key points to remember are:

(1) Pay attention to the position of the foot for each particular kick, noting the striking surface applicable. (See figs 1–5)

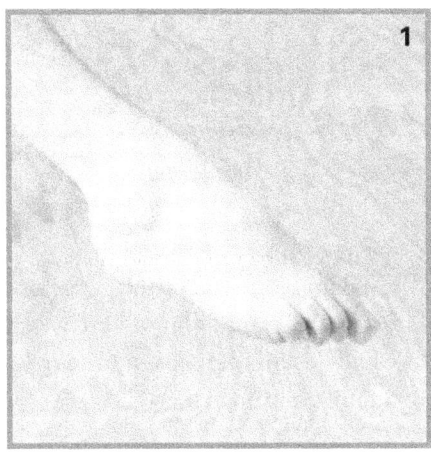

Haisoku (instep)

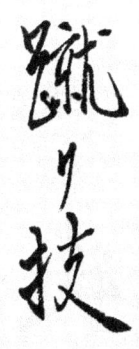

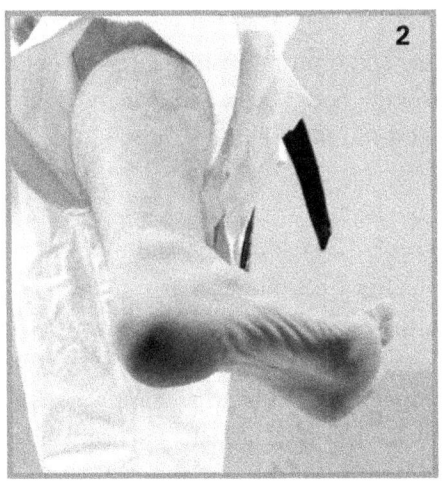

Kakato (heel)

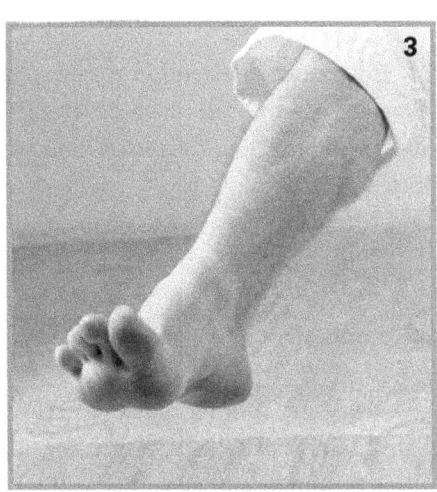

Koshi (ball)

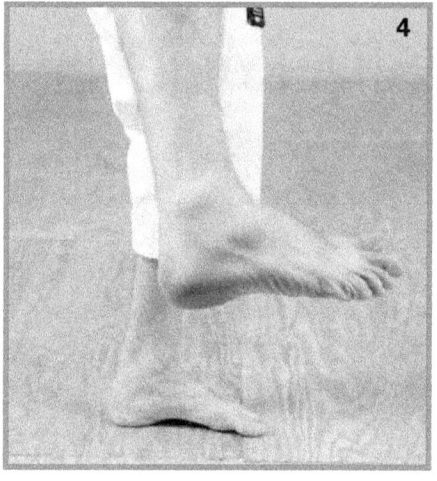
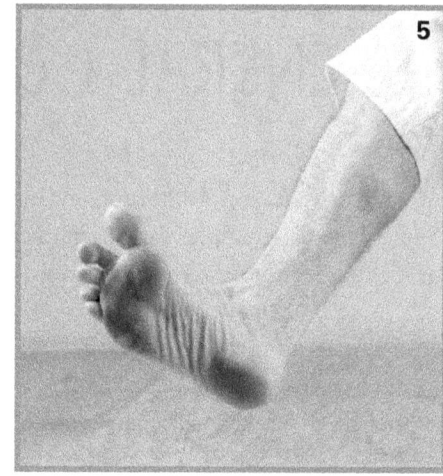

Sokuto (edge)   Teisoku (sole)

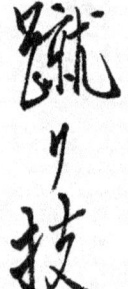

(2) Maximize the use of the entire body when executing the technique. If the kick requires translation of bodyweight, be sure to drive off of the supporting leg. Fully utilize the hips in order to use the whole body efficiently, allowing you to attain a maximal effect.

(3) Speed generates power. Attempt to relax and incorporate a whipping action into the kicks to help to maximize the speed and thus the powerful effect of the kicks.

(4) Pay particular attention to the supporting leg, insuring that it is slightly bent, allowing you to utilize it to drive and control the bodyweight and balance. The supporting leg should be used in an equal and complimentary manner to the kicking leg.

(5) Don't forget to use *hiki ashi*, (snapping back the kicking leg), and to minimize the amount of time that you are on one leg. The quicker that you are able to return to a stance standing on both legs, the less vulnerable you will be.

(6) Always try to utilize kicking techniques together with hand techniques. When you want to kick, punch—when you want to punch, kick. This will allow a free flowing use of all of the techniques in less predictable and more efficient manner.

Explanation of Categories

In an attempt to categorize the methods of utilizing the techniques effectively, the following categories have been established:

Offensive Combinations—*Direct Attacks—Attacking directly and decisively.* Attacking directly and decisively must be done only when one determines there to be an opening (physical, mental or otherwise.) Remember that attacking in such a manner is not to be confused with a *random* or *arbitrary* attack, which is most often unwise with a prepared opponent. Moreover, it is important to remember that when you attack, you are also open to some degree. For the purposes of this book, techniques were necessarily arranged in categories. In effective *kumite*, this manner of attack would more likely be preceded with some type of set up in order to create an opening, rather than the manner of attack described in the sequences here.

Offensive Combinations—*Indirect Attacks—Utilizing feints, set-ups and invitations.* This means of attacking includes feints, set-ups, and inviting your opponent to attack *(sasoi waza)*, so as to expose a weakness or opening in his own defense. This is a very effective and often used manner of attacking.

Defensive Combinations—*Counterattacks using Maai/Tai Sabaki (Distance/shifting).* In this case, two of the most significant principles of *kumite* are utilized in a defensive manner to counterattack. Distance and body shifting allow one to escape an opponent's attack while positioning oneself to counter effectively. Mastery of these principles are essential to the development of *kumite.*

Defensive Combinations—*Counterattacks using Uke Waza (Blocking techniques).* Blocking and counterattacking is another essential principle utilized frequently in karate. It can be used together with counterattacks in a number of ways, with various uses of timing, and in combination with the use of distance and body shifting.

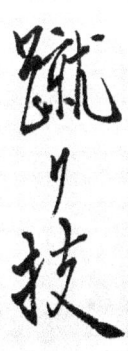

MAE GERI

Mae geri is perhaps the most widely used of all kicking techniques. Though relatively easy to understand, proper execution produces a devastating technique, that when highly refined, is very difficult to stop. Additionally, the kick can be delivered from a variety of angles and distances, and can be used in combination with many other techniques, or to set up many other techniques.

From the initial instant, it is important to drive the knee upward very quickly and strongly. This can be accomplished by starting with "kicking" off the floor with the heel of the foot that is executing the kick. Simultaneously, squeeze the inner thigh muscles of both legs and compress the stomach while exhaling to bring the knee up sharply and decisively, as if to deliver *hiza geri* (knee attack). At this point, the level of the body should not have changed, the kicking foot should be held tight to the buttocks and parallel to the floor, and the bent position of the supporting leg should be at least the same angle as it was when it began while in *zenkutsu dachi*. From here, continue using the momentum and acceleration that has been generated to continue the delivery of the kick, by thrusting your entire bodyweight forward through translation of the hips. Here the supporting leg becomes very important, as it drives the body forward and the kicking leg begins to extend toward the target. It is important not to lean back during the kick, yet to allow the hips to tilt to obtain maximum reach and power. As the kick travels in a slightly upward arcing trajectory and reaches the target, *kime* the back leg while extending the foot, then quickly recoil the leg while compressing the stomach and cutting the breath for a brief instant. The speed of the recoil of the kick should exceed that of the extension. Lastly, as quickly as possible, return the foot to the ground to minimize the amount of time that you are on one leg.

Masterclass Karate

EXECUTION

Note that knee drives directly toward target on linear path.

Hip and bodyweight are thrust forward while support leg is bent.

Mae Geri

Masterclass Karate

COMMON MISTAKES

In this instance (fig 1), the course of the kick is incorrect, as the knee rises upward improperly and late, rather than driving on a linear path to the target. Note that fig 2 shows that the heel of the kicking foot does not begin in a position tight to buttocks. Both errors will result in a net loss of power.

Fig 3—shows the position of the kicking foot with the toes pointing downward as the ankle is extended, interrupting the correct course of the kick on its linear path and preventing the kick from being delivered at a close distance. The only instance in which this foot position would be advantageous would be when delivering the front kick to the groin *(kin-geri)*, on an upward course *(keri-age)*.

Mae Geri

Fig 4—shows the support leg straightening as the kick is chambered, preventing driving off of the support leg to increase the power of the kick. Energy is also lost upward in this case.

Fig 5—shows the shoulder dropping as the kick is initiated, exposing the intention to kick to the opponent, disrupting the balance, and leaving the kicker further open to counter. The kicker's toes are also pointed downward, and the support foot is turned too far outward

ADVANCED/ALTERNATIVE APPLICATION

Fig 1—shows the kick being delivered on a very slightly inward course, similar to that of gyaku mawashi geri, but not as pronounced, making it much more difficult to avoid or block.

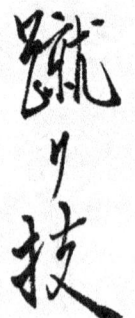

Fig 2—shows the kick being delivered to the opponent's front hip bone, as it arrives under the *kamae* at the closest point of the body as the target.

Fig 3—Alternatively, the kick can be delivered to the chin using the heel rather than the ball of the foot.

Mae Geri

TRAINING EXERCISES

(1) Begin by facing a partner and raising the knee as quickly as possible, then return the kicking leg to ground quickly as if performing *fumikomi*.

Masterclass Karate

(2) A partner presses down slightly on the knee, as shown, for a count of ten seconds per repetition, to strengthen the proper muscles (thigh flexors) and to understand the role of the compression of the stomach.

(3) As your partner holds the ankle of your kicking leg with both hands, explode decisively to bring the knee up quickly to deliver the kick. Repeat 30 times each leg.

Mae Geri

(4) Interlace your fingers under your upper thigh as shown, and slowly extend the leg fully without dropping the knee. Hold for ten seconds.

OFFENSIVE COMBINATIONS
DIRECT ATTACKS—Attacking directly and decisively

(1) Shift the feet slightly to the side, and as your opponent adjusts his position, quickly deliver mae geri to chudan.

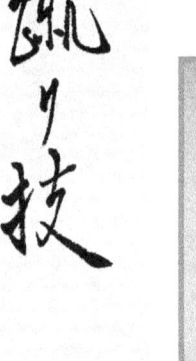

Mae Geri

(2) Step in with the rear leg to reach the optimal distance *(tsurikomi ashi)*, and deliver the kick with the front leg, *(kizami geri)*.

Masterclass Karate

(3) Execute mae geri with the rear leg, and upon realizing that the distance is short, take a small shifting step and again deliver mae geri, with the same leg, as kizami geri.

Mae Geri

INDIRECT ATTACKS—*Utilizing feints, set-ups, and invitations*

(1) Execute a strong jodan attack or feint to jodan with kizami zuki to your opponent's face in order to bring his attention and response upward, while simultaneously sliding your front foot back slightly to adjust the distance for the mae geri to follow. Alternatively, the front foot can slide in, in order to create the proper distance or angle, depending upon the reaction of your opponent.

Slide forward or back

Masterclass Karate

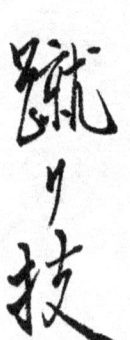

(2) Take a quick short step forward to feint an attack and to cause your opponent to step back. You can also do this by simultaneously feigning jodan zuki by delivering a shortened punch. Just as he regains his balance while recovering and begins to move back in, execute mae geri. This requires great understanding of timing in order to disrupt his rhythm and balance.

Mae Geri

Masterclass Karate

(3) Entice your opponent to attack by creating an opening in your kamae, as shown. The amount should be just enough that your opponent believes it to be a real opening and not a trap. As he attacks with gyaku zuki, block with osae uke while at the same time delivering jodan uraken. As he retreats to escape, execute mae geri to finish.

Mae Geri

DEFENSIVE COMBINATIONS
COUNTERATTACKS USING MAAI/TAI SABAKI (Distance/shifting)

(1) Counter your opponent's mae geri by first executing *ashikomi* (fig 2) in order to escape the distance, thus avoiding the kick. The moment your feet come together, shift your weight and twist your hips immediately as you follow with your own mae geri, as shown in figs 3–5. Your kick should reach its target before your opponent can completely recoil his kick, and you finish by facing your opponent at an angle to prevent a second attack.

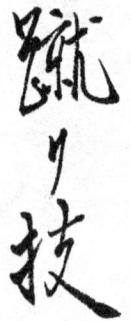

Mae Geri

前蹴り

Masterclass Karate

(2) Shift to the side and at an angle as shown to avoid jodan mawashi geri. As you land in neko ashi dachi, immediately execute kizami mae geri before your opponent's kicking leg lands.

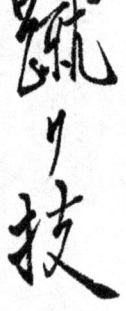

Mae Geri

Reverse Angle

Masterclass Karate

COUNTERATTACKS USING UKE WAZA (Blocking techniques)

(1) Counter your opponent's kizami zuki by shifting to the side while simultaneously blocking the punch and executing kizami mae geri to the floating ribs.

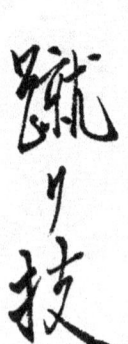

Mae Geri

(2) As your opponent attacks with chudan gyaku zuki, use gedan barai to deflect the punch, while simultaneously shifting your front foot back and twisting the hips so that you are facing him on an angle. Then, as he follows with kizami zuki, angle your body slightly and deliver mae geri to the left side of his ribs.

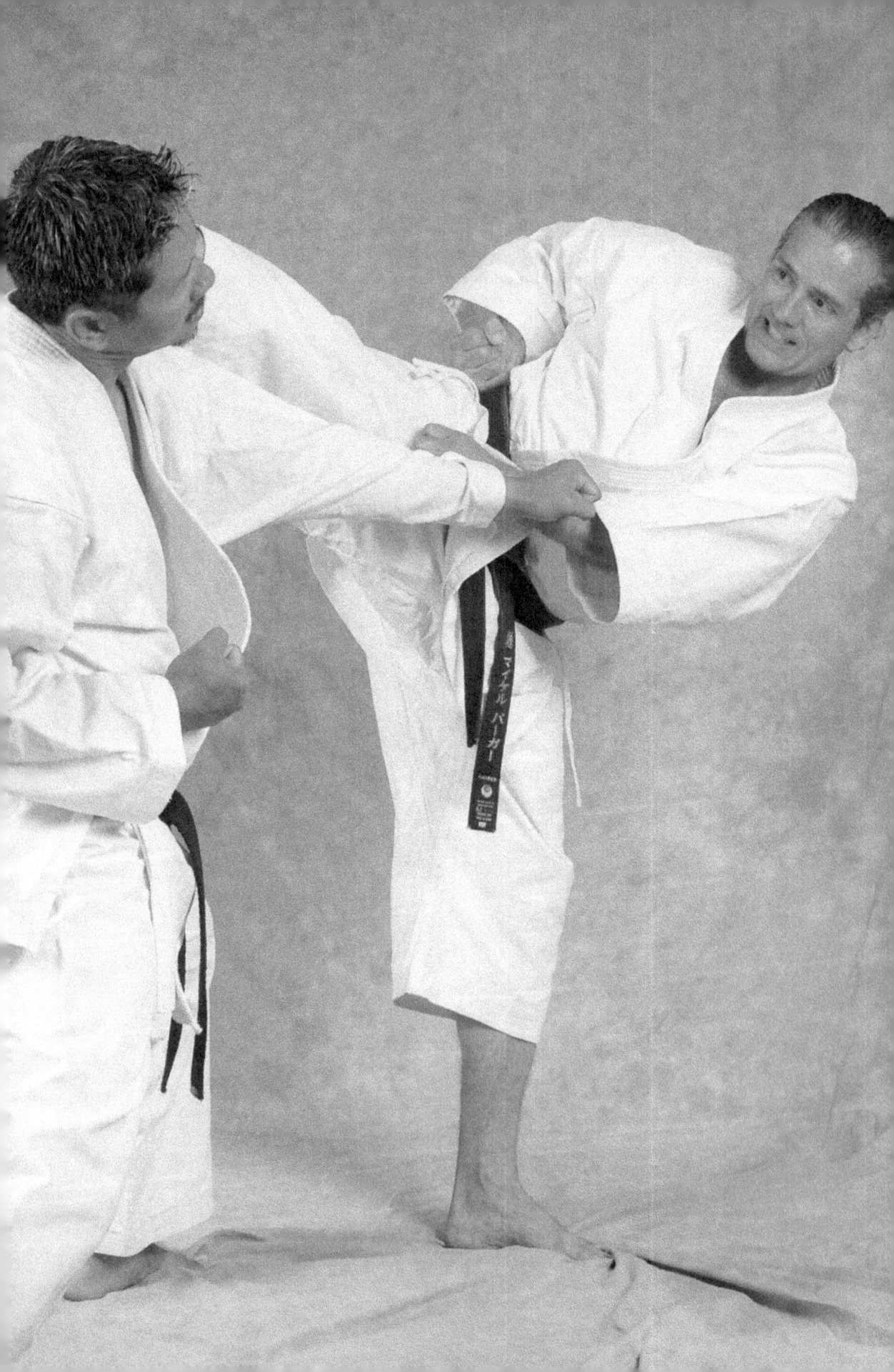

Mawashi Geri

Mawashi geri (roundhouse kick) is unique in that it can be delivered from a variety of angles and distances, and the course of the kick, position of the foot upon impact, and direction of the kick are all highly adaptable to circumstances. Mawashi geri, properly delivered, can come from outside an opponent's field of peripheral vision, and can go around blocks or come from angles difficult to block. Additionally, the power generated by twisting the body into the technique at the right moment makes this a devastating technique.

Fundamentally speaking, mawashi geri should be learned initially as a large motion incorporating the full rotation of the hips, in order that one understands the mechanics involved relative to the generation of power. At more advanced levels, the course of the kick can be modified (see advanced application) to allow for quicker delivery and a more protected, less predicable attack.

Begin by bringing the kicking leg out to the side of the body, parallel to the ground, keeping the heel close to the buttocks, support leg bending, and body upright. Maintaining a bent supporting leg throughout insures maximum height, reach, and balance, by allowing for unrestricted use of the hips, as well as keeping a lower center of gravity. Now, rotate the hips with the kicking leg and deliver the kick describing a wide arc. If the designated target is jodan, the kick can be delivered on a slightly downward angle, making it nearly impossible to block. The striking surface of the foot can be either that of *haisoku* (instep) or *koshi* (ball of foot). The supportive foot should be allowed to slide naturally on the floor as the body rotates. This will not only allow the body to rotate freely, but will also prevent a potential knee or ankle injury.

Masterclass Karate

EXECUTION

1

2

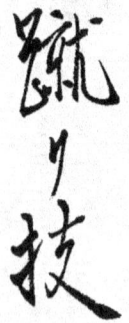

3

Mawashi Geri

Masterclass Karate

EXECUTION—Front View

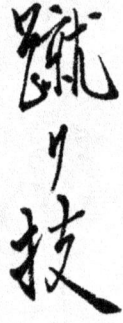

Mawashi Geri

Masterclass Karate

COMMON MISTAKES

In figs. 1 & 2 the course of the kick is incorrect, resulting in the kick being delivered obliquely on an upward course. It is therefore more likely to strike the target indirectly with a glancing blow, is more easily avoided, and lacks maximal power.

Fig 2—shows the hips not being rotated fully with the kick, again resulting in a tremendous loss of power and reach, with the entire body not being utilized fully as described previously.

Fig 3—as the kick is chambered, the heel is not tight to the buttocks, which will result in a loss of power as the kick is delivered.

ADVANCED/ ALTERNATIVE APPLICATION

Once the principals of generating power through proper use of the body are mastered, experienced practitioners can modify the course of the kick slightly, beginning on a shorter course, giving the initial appearance of *mae geri*, and then suddenly changing the course of the kick at the last moment. Power can be retained by full hip rotation and the downward trajectory can be utilized in the same manner as described previously. This manner of delivery is also faster and provides for a more covered position during the initial stages of execution.

Masterclass Karate

TRAINING EXERCISES

1. While seated on the floor as shown, practice the course and develop the strength and flexibility of the hips.

Mawashi Geri

2. One can then practice while performing the kick slowly by the count while in zenkutsu dachi, before proceeding more quickly.

3. Similarly, practice against a wall by the count, as shown.

Mawashi Geri

Masterclass Karate

4. The same kind of practice is essential with a partner holding wrists, in order to gain an understanding of target, distance, and trajectory.

Mawashi Geri

5. Partner drills—one person executes the kick off both front and back legs to partner's open hands in juji uke position, and then each partner attacks simultaneously to the body, as shown, holding the arms high.

Mawashi Geri

6. Mawashi geri from zenkutsu dachi, not directly to the front, but 45 degrees left past the front midline of the body. This exercise emphasizes the full rotation of the hips.

Masterclass Karate

OFFENSIVE COMBINATIONS
DIRECT ATTACKS—Attacking directly and decisively

(1) Perform a slight step back quickly (*ashi komi*) to change feet, then immediately use your rear leg to deliver mawashi geri to the head of your opponent.

Mawashi Geri

Masterclass Karate

(2) Execute a quick mawashi geri to gedan level in order to bring the attention of your opponent downward, then follow quickly with the same leg to jodan level attack. The jodan attack must follow instantly to insure success.

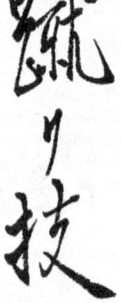

Mawashi Geri

二

回し蹴り

Masterclass Karate

(3) Begin by executing gyaku zuki to your opponent's body, then follow immediately with mawashi geri to jodan, followed by another gyaku zuki.

Mawashi Geri

INDIRECT ATTACKS—*Using feints, set-ups, and invitations*

(1) Begin by kicking with mawashi geri to your opponent's head. As his attention shifts to block and avoid the upper level attack, recoil completely and use the same leg to execute yoko geri kekomi to his body.

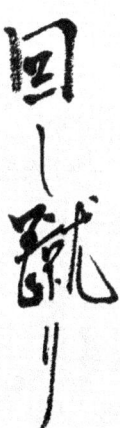

Masterclass Karate

(2) Entice your opponent to attack with mae geri by creating an opening in your defense. As he attacks, slide your front foot back and laterally in order to evade the attack arriving in heisoku dachi (dependant upon the distance); then deliver an immediate mawashi geri to his head with the front foot before his leg touches the ground.

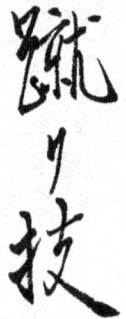

Mawashi Geri

DEFENSIVE COMBINATIONS
COUNTERATTACKS USING MAAI/TAI SABAKI (Distance/shifting)

(1) As your opponent attacks with kizami zuki, shift to the side while parrying the punch as shown, then, just as your foot lands, use the floor as a springboard to accelerate your kicking leg, delivering a quick mawashi geri to the back of his head.

(2) Your opponent attacks with kizami zuki, then steps in quickly with jodan oizuki. Parry his initial punch with you rear hand while sliding slightly backward, then, as he steps deeply to attack again, slip his punch by stepping to the side with your front foot and moving your head to allow his attack to pass by. At the same instant, deliver mawashi geri to his throat. Finish by reaping his front foot with the same leg, and as he lands, delivering *fumikomi* (stomping attack).

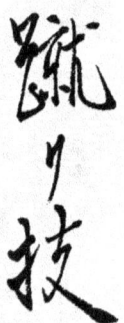

Mawashi Geri

Masterclass Karate

(3) Begin by creating an opening for your opponent by raising your lead hand slightly so as to expose your body. As your opponent initiates an attack with gyaku zuki, respond by intuiting his attack and at the same instant deliver kizami mawashi geri to jodan. In this instance, it is important to remain covered and able to block in the event your timing is not precise.

Mawashi Geri

回し蹴り

Masterclass Karate

COUNTERATTACKS USING UKE WAZA (Blocking techniques)

(1) Your opponent faces you as shown, then attacks with mae geri, followed by a reverse punch toward your head. Block his kick with gedan barai, while at the same time shifting your rear foot slightly and changing your stance as shown to change the distance and angle. Now, as his punch arrives well short of the target, seize his arm and spring quickly off of your rear leg and deliver mawashi geri to the side or back of his head. Note that by changing the angle from which you attack distance and target are changed accordingly.

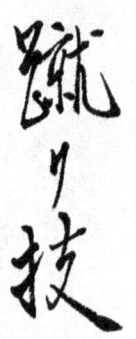

Mawashi Geri

Masterclass Karate

(2) As your opponent attacks with gyaku zuki, use your lead hand to execute an open handed pressing block (osae uke), while simultaneously delivering gyaku zuki. This serves to unbalance and position the head of your opponent into the proper distance for the counter. More importantly, just as his lead foot slides into position, and while you are simultaneously blocking/countering, execute a quick sweeping technique with your lead leg to upset his balance. This places your opponent in perfect position for a rapid counter. Follow instantly by using the same leg to deliver mawashi geri to his head.

Mawashi Geri

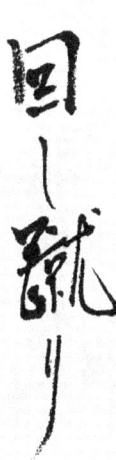

Masterclass Karate

(3) Begin by punching with gyaku zuki toward your opponents head. As he blocks with age uke and counters with gyaku zuki, use your rear hand to parry the punch to the inside while simultaneously spinning to deliver shuto uchi as he retreats. Noticing that he continues to retreat, follow immediately with jodan mawashi geri. Alternatively, spin back to your original position while delivering another shuto uchi, and follow then with mawashi geri to the head.

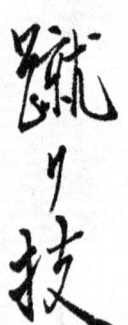

Mawashi Geri

Gyaku Mawashi Geri

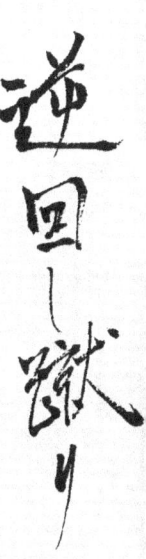

Gyaku mawashi geri (reverse or inside roundhouse kick) is a seldom used but extremely effective kick, and is very difficult to block or evade. It is delivered on an unusual angle, making it very difficult to escape, and when executed properly, has great power and effect.

Gyaku mawashi geri begins in the same manner as mae geri, by chambering the kick with knee high to the chest. From there, however, the course of delivery is changed by changing the position of the knee to allow the leg to become parallel to ground, in the opposite direction of mawashi geri. As the kick is delivered to either jodan or chudan, it becomes nearly impossible to evade or block as it comes from the inside out. As is the case in mawashi geri, either the instep or the ball of the foot can be used as the striking surface.

Masterclass Karate

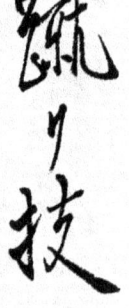

Gyaku Mawashi Geri

Masterclass Karate

COMMON MISTAKES

Fig 1—in this example, the course of the kick is not flat enough, limiting the effect and unique angle of the kick that defines it.

Fig 2—here the practitioner has dropped his hands and changed the level of his shoulders in an attempt to properly deliver the kick, thus giving away his intention and further opening himself to an opponent's attack.

Gyaku Mawashi Geri

TRAINING EXERCISES

(1) Sit as shown to facilitate stretching of the associated areas of the thigh (iliotibial [IT] band) while on the floor. Increasing the flexibility of this tendinous sheath and the associated muscles will enable a better angle of delivery, necessary for proper execution of the kick.

(2) Stretching in butterfly position will also assist to maximize the hip flexibility necessary for proper delivery.

Masterclass Karate

(3) Bringing leg to mae geri position, and then changing the plane of delivery slowly will help to develop the proper muscle groups necessary for optimal delivery.

Gyaku Mawashi Geri

OFFENSIVE COMBINATIONS
DIRECT ATTACKS—Attacking directly and decisively

1. Face your opponent and initiate gyaku mawashi geri to chudan. Follow quickly with mawashi geri to chudan or jodan level. It is important to fully utilize the quick snapping action of the hips in this instance to maximize the effect of the technique.

Masterclass Karate

2. Initiate an attack by executing gyaku mawashi geri, then as your opponent responds, change suddenly to inside ashi barai, as shown. Note that the upper body is also involved in the final counter, as demonstrated here.

Gyaku Mawashi Geri

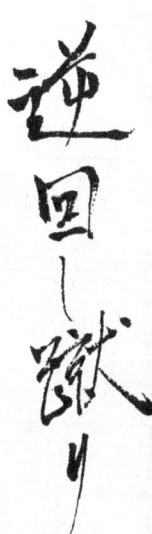

Masterclass Karate

INDIRECT ATTACKS—*Utilizing feints, set-ups, and invitations*

(1) As you initiate an attack to sweep your opponent's leg, he responds by stepping back to avoid the sweep. Quickly, without hesitation, use the same leg to attack with gyaku mawashi geri.

Gyaku Mawashi Geri

Masterclass Karate

(2) Initiate by bringing your knee up quickly to deliver mae geri. Then, as you see your opponent preparing to respond with gedan barai to block the kick, change the course of the kick at the last moment and execute gyaku mawashi geri inside of his block.

Gyaku Mawashi Geri

逆回し蹴り

Masterclass Karate

DEFENSIVE COMBINATIONS
COUNTERATTACKS USING MAAI/TAI SABAKI (Distance/shifting)

(1) When your opponent delivers uraken while sliding toward you, shift both feet to the side and deliver gyaku mawashi geri to the kidney region, using either the instep or the ball of your foot.

Gyaku Mawashi Geri

(2) Similarly, as your opponent steps in attacking with oizuki, anticipate the attack and deliver gyaku mawashi geri before he can complete the attack.

Masterclass Karate

COUNTERATTACKS USING UKE WAZA (Blocking techniques)

(1) As your opponent attacks with kizami zuki, counter with gyaku mawashi geri to chudan while sliding laterally and evading the attack. You can slide to either side and at various angles, dependant upon the distance.

Gyaku Mawashi Geri

(2) Slide laterally while blocking your opponent's mae geri attack with gyaku gedan barai, then respond by delivering gyaku mawashi geri with your rear leg to chudan, as shown.

Ura Mawashi Geri

Ura mawashi geri (hook kick) has become more popular recently, due to the changes in tournament rules by some organizations that encourage more jodan geri. An advanced and difficult kick to master, ura mawashi geri, when delivered with accuracy, can be a devastating attack difficult to stop. It is somewhat limited, however, in its range of uses, and must be delivered with great accuracy to maximize its effect. It can be delivered either to the body or the head, and from either a frontal facing or turning/spinning position. Turning and spinning to deliver the kick increases the power by incorporating an element of centrifugal force, but increases the danger by exposing one's back to the opponent. The striking surface of the foot is generally the heel, but the sole of the foot can also be used, particularly during training to minimize injury.

When facing your opponent, begin by chambering the leg as in mae geri, with the knee slightly to the outside. From there, tilt and rotate the hips, allowing the supporting foot to slide naturally. While keeping your eyes focused on your opponent with your body basically upright, hook the leg from the outside in on a slightly downward course, using the power of the hamstrings (primary leg flexors). The back of the heel reaches the target as the body contracts to a covered position as the kick is completed.

When executing a spinning motion with delivery (ushiro mawashi geri), be sure to turn quickly and strongly to maximize the centrifugal force that can be generated to increase the power of the technique.

Masterclass Karate

Execution

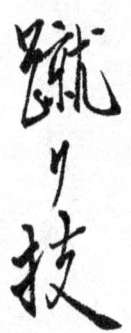

Ura Mawashi Geri

Masterclass Karate

COMMON MISTAKES

Be sure that the arcing, circular aspect of the kick is not too small, which will minimize the effect by restricting the generation of power.

Additionally, this photo (1) shows that the kicker is leaning back and has lost his balance along with visual contact with his target, making it difficult to finish the technique.

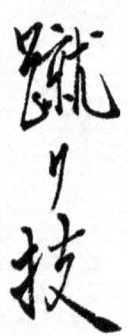

Ura Mawashi Geri

TRAINING EXERCISES

(1) Hold your partner's wrists while facing each other in a fighting stance, then practice the course and angle of the kick while pulling your partners head forward to expose his neck. Alternatively, practice kicking to his back with the sole of your foot.

Masterclass Karate

OFFENSIVE COMBINATIONS
DIRECT ATTACKS—Attacking directly and decisively

(1) Begin by executing gyaku zuki decisively to your opponent's body, anticipating his ability to block. Then, as your opponent responds by evading and blocking the attack, deliver ura mawashi geri to the back of his neck as shown.

Ura Mawashi Geri

INDIRECT ATTACKS—*Utilizing feints, set-ups, and invitations*

(1) Begin by attacking with gyaku zuki followed by ashi barai with your rear leg. As your opponent recognizes your intention, he steps back with his front foot in order to avoid being swept, then begins to counter by stepping in with a punch aimed at your head. Before he can complete the punch, immediately execute ura mawashi geri to jodan (fig 5).

Masterclass Karate

DEFENSIVE COMBINATIONS
COUNTERATTACKS USING MAAI/TAI SABAKI (Distance/shifting)

(1) Your opponent attacks with kizami zuki/oizuki. Slide back far to avoid the kizami, then as he steps forward to punch, evade the punch by moving slightly to the side while at the same time stepping through to deliver ura mawashi geri to the back of his head.

Ura Mawashi Geri

裏回し蹴り

Masterclass Karate

COUNTERATTACKS USING UKE WAZA (Blocking techniques)

(1) Noticing that your opponent's tendency is to attack with gyaku zuki, you set up in gyaku kamae as shown, giving him an opening to attack. As he attacks chudan gyaku zuki, shift laterally while simultaneously parrying his attack with an obliquely angled shuto uke. Follow instantaneously with ura mawashi geri to back of his head or neck.

Ura Mawashi Geri

Masterclass Karate

(2) Your opponent delivers a combination, kizami zuki/mae geri/gyaku zuki. Parry his kizami zuki with your rear hand, then as he attempts to follow with the ensuing mae geri, step slightly the side and block the kick with shuto uke on an oblique plane to redirect the kick. Immediately use your back leg to counter with ura mawashi geri to the back of his neck before his gyaku zuki can be fully executed.

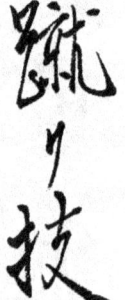

Ura Mawashi Geri

Masterclass Karate

(3) As your opponent delivers kizami mawashi geri toward your head, parry the kick with your open hand while simultaneously spinning out of the way to the opposite side and deliver ura mawashi geri to his neck or collarbone. Perfect timing must be used to make this technique effective.

Ura Mawashi Geri

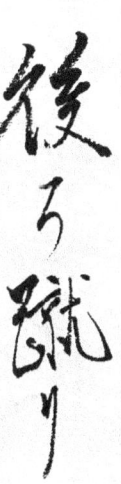

Ushiro Geri

Ushiro geri (back kick), is an extremely powerful technique that can be very difficult to stop when executed properly and decisively. It has tremendous thrusting and penetrating power, and can be used in a variety of situations at both close and far distances. Mastery of the turn is a critical point, as turning the back on an opponent can have unfavorable results if not done quickly and decisively.

Begin by keeping your eyes on your opponent and sharply twisting the hips, while at the same time squeezing both legs together, and at the last moment, turning the head to view your target. It is important that you arrive in this position with the knees bent. The kick thrusts outward immediately following the raising of the knee, as the inner thighs squeeze past each other and the support leg drives the kicking leg to the target. The toes should be pointed at about a 30 degree angle downward to allow for full unrestricted use of the hips, while the legs are spread fully, until finally, impact is made with the heel (kakato) of the kicking foot. The position of angling the upper body can be modified according to the height of the kick and distance of the opponent.

Masterclass Karate

EXECUTION

Ushiro Geri

COMMON MISTAKES

Fig 1—The inner thighs of the kicker's legs do not pass closely by each other, resulting in the kick not being delivered in a linear path, but rather one that has a circular element. Balance, delivery, and power are thus compromised accordingly, and the kick is not effective.

Fig 2—In addition to the legs being separated, the position of the foot during execution is incorrect, as the toes are pointing too far laterally, making the kick more like yoko geri kekomi, a different technique.

Ushiro Geri

TRAINING EXERCISES

(1) Practice arriving at the position of delivery by squeezing your legs together and turning quickly to land in heisoku dachi. Return quickly with the same energy. Repeat.

(2) From here, now practice with a partner, giving special attention to the latter part of the delivery, bringing your knee high before extending the kick to various levels. Note that the body position can be adjusted accordingly, even as much as so as to finish in a parallel position, depending on the height of the kick, as shown.

Jodan level

Ushiro Geri

Masterclass Karate

(3) Deliver the kick in three counts, as shown (Series A), landing finally in zenkutsu dachi as shown. From here use your front leg to deliver ushiro geri to the rear so you end once again in your beginning position (Series B). Repeat.

SERIES A

1

2

3

4

Ushiro Geri

SERIES B

Masterclass Karate

OFFENSIVE COMBINATIONS
DIRECT ATTACKS—Attacking directly and decisively

(1) Begin by executing jodan gyaku zuki to your opponents face. As he shifts his weight slightly to avoid the punch, follow immediately with ashi barai, causing him to step backwards. As he attempts to counter, immediately follow with ushiro geri with either leg.

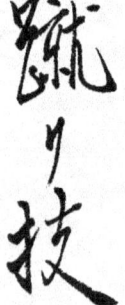

Ushiro Geri

Masterclass Karate

(2) Seize the initiative by attacking, sliding in with gyaku zuki to drive your opponent back, then pause for a brief instant, and as he reacts to counter by moving in forward with kizami zuki, use your front hand to block and turn quickly and meet his momentum as you deliver ushiro geri. Alternatively, feint with the gyaku zuki to invite your opponent's counter with kizami zuki. As he does so, again use your front hand to block while spinning to deliver ushiro geri.

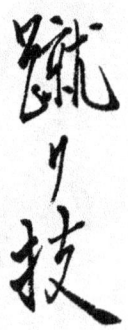

Ushiro Geri

Masterclass Karate

INDIRECT ATTACKS—Utilizing feints, set-ups, and invitations

(1) Invite your opponent to attack with gyaku zuki by momentarily dropping your lead hand to your side, as shown. As he attacks, use the same arm to block as you spin to deliver ushiro geri.

Ushiro Geri

Masterclass Karate

(2) Take a short, quick step forward, maintaining your kamae, to gage your opponents reaction. If he responds by retreating as shown, turn decisively while taking a deeper step toward him with your rear leg, then execute ushiro geri (Series 1). If he does not respond by escaping, immediately execute the technique with the rear leg without taking the additional step (Series 2).

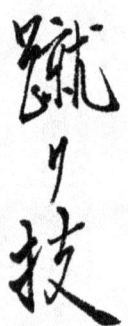

SERIES 1

1

2

Ushiro Geri

Masterclass Karate

SERIES 2

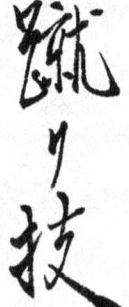

Ushiro Geri

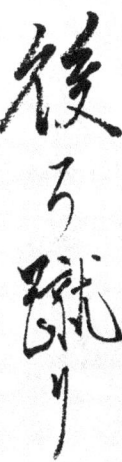

Masterclass Karate

DEFENSIVE COMBINATIONS
COUNTERATTACKS USING MAAI/TAI SABAKI (Distance/shifting)

(1) Anticipate your opponents stepping attack toward to your head, by timing his attack and turning quickly to deliver ushiro geri to ribs as he moves forward with the punch.

Note that the near parallel position of the body helps to prevent you from being attacked.

Ushiro Geri

Masterclass Karate

(2) As your opponent attacks with gyaku zuki and follows with mawashi geri, slide back slightly to avoid the punch, then step back with your front foot and land momentarily in zenkutsu dachi facing 180 degrees away from your opponent with your body leaning forward. Then, with your eyes still in contact with your target, turn quickly to deliver ushiro geri just before his foot lands.

Ushiro Geri

Masterclass Karate

COUNTERATTACKS USING UKE WAZA (Blocking techniques)

(1) At close distance, counter your opponent's kizami zuki by parrying the punch with your lead hand while at the same time turning quickly to deliver a low ushiro geri to the groin or lower abdomen.

Ushiro Geri

Yoko Geri Kekomi

Yoko geri can be delivered either by thrusting, as in the case of *yoko geri kekomi* or by snapping, described as *yoko geri keage*.

Yoko geri kekomi is a powerful and penetrating technique, delivered in a linear fashion primarily with the heel as the striking surface. It has excellent stopping power, and can be delivered to both high and low target areas from various stances, usually from mid to long ranges of distance.

The kick is initiated by chambering the kicking leg as if to do mae geri, with the knee high, toes back, and foot parallel to the ground. From here, the knee is shifted so that the lower leg becomes parallel as it is prepared to be thrust linearly toward the target. At impact, it is important to note that the hips are extended while pushing off of the supporting leg. The body should remain as upright as possible, with the heel up and toes pulled back and down slightly toward the ground. Allow the supporting foot to pivot naturally as the kick is delivered, while keeping as much of the foot as possible on the ground. This will allow for free extension of the kick and reduce the risk of possible knee or ankle joint injury to the supportive leg. Be sure to kime the entire body strongly at impact, before returning the kicking leg along the same course and then quickly to the ground, maintaining a covered position throughout.

Masterclass Karate

EXECUTION

Yoko Geri Kekomi

Masterclass Karate

EXECUTION—Front View

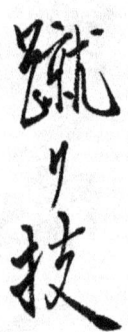

Yoko Geri Kekomi

COMMON MISTAKES

Fig 1—The course of the kick here has too much of an arcing element and is thus more akin to *yoko geri keage*, as the linear aspect that leads to penetration is compromised.

Incorrect Position

Fig 2—Shows an improper position of the foot at impact. This is a result of not fully rotating the leg and extending the hips into the kick, minimizing power and distance of the kick.

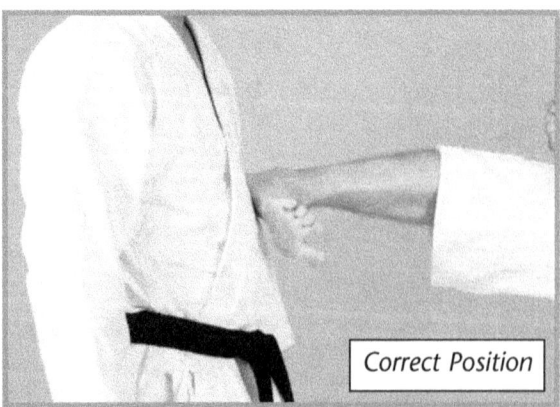

Correct Position

Yoko Geri Kekomi

Fig 3—The kicker is leaning his body too much away from the kick, compromising the power of the kick at impact by not fully utilizing his body.

Masterclass Karate

TRAINING EXERCISES

(1) Standing against a wall or in heisoku dachi, perform the kick slowly in four counts (as shown), holding each position for a ten second count to strengthen the associated muscle groups. (Be sure to pay close attention to balance and body position at every given moment during delivery.)

Yoko Geri Kekomi

Masterclass Karate

(2) Use your front leg to deliver kizami geri, maintaining the forward thrust off the back leg, then follow quickly with the same kick off the back leg. As you land forward in zenkutsu dachi, step through turning 180 degrees, facing the opposite direction. Repeat.

Kizami yoko geri kekomi

Yoko Geri Kekomi

Followed by rear leg attack.

Finish facing 180°

Masterclass Karate

OFFENSIVE COMBINATIONS
DIRECT ATTACKS—Attacking directly and decisively

(1) Initiate an attack by executing gyaku zuki and ashi barai, as shown in fig 1. As your opponent responds to counter, use the same leg to deliver yoko kekomi to his ribs.

Yoko Geri Kekomi

Masterclass Karate

(2) Step forward decisively while delivering a high back fist strike to your opponents head. As your attacking hand recoils, bring your rear foot forward so as to land in kosa dachi at an angle to your opponent. Noting that his hands have risen to avoid the first attack, you now have a clear opening to attack with yoko geri kekomi.

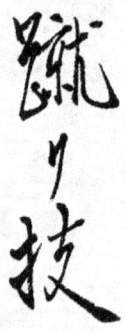

Yoko Geri Kekomi

Masterclass Karate

INDIRECT ATTACKS—Utilizing feints, set-ups, and invitations

(1) Use your open hand to move your opponents lead hand slightly to the side, following immediately with age zuki (rising punch) toward his face, while at the same time moving forward. Then, as you step and deliver another gyaku zuki to his face, land with your front foot perpendicular as shown, following with the rear leg execution of yoko geri kekomi.

Note that the initial opening is an excellent set-up for numerous techniques.

Yoko Geri Kekomi

横蹴り蹴込み

Masterclass Karate

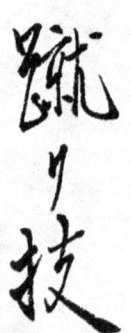

(2) Feint with a short kizami zuki, inviting your opponent to counter with gyaku zuki. As he does so, block his counter with the same hand while at the same time sliding your front foot back slightly and punching to face with gyaku zuki. Now, as his attention turns to protecting his head, use your back leg to execute yoko geri kekomi.

Yoko Geri Kekomi

Masterclass Karate

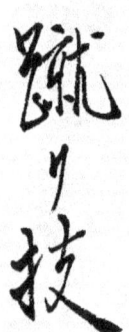

DEFENSIVE COMBINATIONS
COUNTERATTACKS USING MAAI/TAI SABAKI (Distance/shifting)

(1) As your opponent attacks with kizami zuki, use your lead leg to quickly counter with *kizami yoko geri kekomi*.

Yoko Geri Kekomi

(2) Shift to the side slightly using *tai-sabaki* and changing your stance to evade your opponent's *mae geri* as shown, then quickly counter with *yoko geri kekomi* to the throat with your front leg as he recoils the missed kick and tries to deliver *jodan zuki*.

Masterclass Karate

COUNTERATTACKS USING UKE WAZA (Blocking techniques)

(1) Your opponent attacks with *jodan uraken uchi* (backfist strike) to your head, and then follows with side thrust kick. Evade the initial strike by sliding back out of range, then step back at angle while blocking his kick with *soto uke*. Follow immediately by delivering *yoko geri kekomi* with your front leg.

Yoko Geri Kekomi

(2) As your opponent attacks with mae geri and follows with a punch with either hand to your head, shift your rear foot laterally and block his kick with gedan barai while changing your stance so that you land in zenkutsu dachi at an angle, as shown. As he attempts to follow with a punch, use uraken to block his attack. Follow instantly to force him to retreat, then take a crossing step and execute yoko geri kekomi.

Yoko Geri Keage

Yoko geri keage differs from *yoko geri kekomi* in several ways: not only are mechanics and the course of kick different, but the kick generates a different type of shocking energy at impact. Accordingly, the target areas should be selected so as to allow the maximum efficiency of this type of energy. Typical targets include floating ribs, throat and chin, groin, and knees. *Yoko geri keage* can be executed at all distances, and can be used to effectively block attacks as well.

Contrary to the chambering of yoko geri kekomi, yoko geri keage begins by raising the knee at a 45 degree angle in front of the body. The kick continues toward the target on an upward arcing course, until it makes impact using the blade edge of the foot *(sokuto)* with a sharp, snapping shock before being quickly pulled back to the chambered position. It is especially important to relax the leg and hip joints during delivery, facilitating the necessary whip-like snapping action of the leg that provides for maximum effect. Proper understanding of contraction and expansion of the body is also essential.

Masterclass Karate

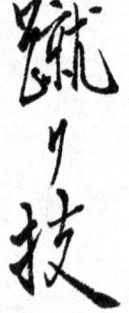

EXECUTION

Yoko Geri Keage

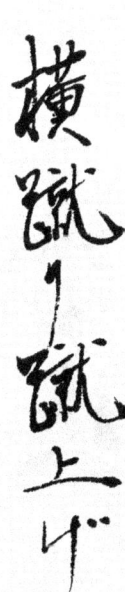

COMMON MISTAKES

Fig 1—This example shows the kicking leg being chambered with the knee too far laterally, exceeding the stated 45 degree angle, resulting in a kick that more closely resembles mae geri. Note also that the position of the foot is also incorrect, with the toes facing upward, preventing proper delivery.

Fig 2—Here the kick is not recoiled properly, but rather is dropped to the ground before recoiling back to original chambered position at the inner thigh.

TRAINING EXERCISES

(1) Begin by holding your foot as shown with the sole of the foot facing upward and the knee relaxed, support leg bending. Let go with your hand and allow the leg to flick out quickly, concentrating almost entirely on the recoil as you catch the foot again with your hand. Repeat, while slowly increasing the height of the kick. This exercise will help one understand the whip-like flicking action of the kick.

2. From *heisoku dachi*, use one leg to repeatedly to deliver *yoko geri keage*, first low, then to a medium height, then higher. Attention should be given to minimize leaning the body to the side.

Masterclass Karate

OFFENSIVE COMBINATIONS
DIRECT ATTACKS—Attacking directly and decisively

(1) Shift both feet quickly to the side so as to face your opponent at a 45 degree angle, then before he can complete his adjustment to face you, attack strongly with yoko geri keage with your front leg to his ribcage.

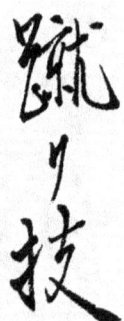

Yoko Geri Keage

横蹴り蹴上げ

Masterclass Karate

(2) Begin by chambering your leg as if to deliver mae geri, then as your opponent anticipates that attack and turns his attention to cover a chudan level attack, redirect your attack slightly to attack under his chin with yoko geri keage, as shown.

Yoko Geri Keage

Masterclass Karate

INDIRECT ATTACKS—Utilizing feints, set-ups, and invitations

(1) Invite your opponent to attack by stepping in slightly with your rear leg to change to distance, then as he begins to counter with gyaku zuki, quickly pull your front foot back at an angle and immediately deliver yoko geri keage to his armpit with your opposite leg.

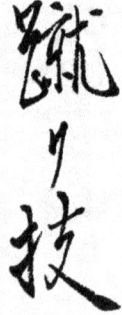

Yoko Geri Keage

七

横蹴り蹴上げ

Masterclass Karate

(2) Feint with gyaku zuki while at the same time taking a quick half step forward with your rear leg. As your opponent responds with jodan kizami zuki, change the angle of your body while blocking his punch with your own nagashi kizami zuki, as shown. Follow immediately with yoko geri keage to his exposed ribcage.

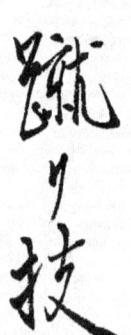

Yoko Geri Keage

DEFENSIVE COMBINATIONS
COUNTERATTACKS USING MAAI/TAI SABAKI (Distance/shifting)

(1) Shift slightly to the side while blocking your opponent's mae geri, and catch his heel while twisting your hips to gyaku hanmi position. Then follow quickly with yoko geri keage to the groin.

Yoko Geri Keage

COUNTERATTACKS USING UKE WAZA (Blocking techniques)

(1) Using mikazuki geri to parry your opponent's mae geri attack, follow with the same leg executing yoko geri keage, as shown here.

Less Frequently Used Kicks

MAE GERI KEKOMI (Front Thrust Kick)

DESCRIPTION

Mae geri kekomi is a devastating and powerful technique that can be effectively delivered to the *jodan, chudan,* or *gedan* level. It is particularly useful to use the heel to strike when attacking the chin, throat, or the knee. Alternatively, the ball of the foot can be used effectively to penetrate the target as well, particularly to *chudan* level.

Begin by chambering the kicking leg in the same fashion as if to deliver mae geri, then thrusting the leg forward on a linear path, use the heel or the ball of the foot to penetrate the designated target. Be sure to fully utilize the extension of the hip during delivery of the kick, using proper *kime* at the moment of impact to penetrate the target before recoiling the kick and returning the foot to the ground decisively. *Mae geri kekomi* differs from *keage* in that the course is one that is more linear in nature, whereas *keage* has an arcing trajectory. One should note the differences in *maai* (distance) when using the heel versus the ball of the foot for execution, as well as the results of impact.

Masterclass Karate

APPLICATION

In the examples shown, note the attacks to jodan, chudan and gedan levels. In all cases, penetration of the kick is maximized by utilizing the hips, support leg and kime properly.

OTOSHI GERI (Axe Kick)

DESCRIPTION

Otoshi geri, commonly referred to in English as "axe-kick" has somewhat limited use, but is extremely effective when dropping from above to attack the head, collarbone, or back of the opponent.

It is executed by first swinging the leg upward decisively, above the desired target, then forcefully pulling the leg down with the knee slightly bent, utilizing the muscles responsible for extension of the thigh. By using the heel as the striking surface, great force can be generated to attack downwardly to an opponent who is either standing or has fallen, as shown.

APPLICATION

The accompanying photos show various applications of otoshi geri.

Attacking an opponent on the ground.

Attacking the shoulder or neck.

Attacking the arms to destroy opponent's kamae.

MIKAZUKI GERI (Crescent Kick)

DESCRIPTION

Mikazuki geri, known more commonly known as *"crescent kick"* is seen in many of the Shotokan kata, and is useful both offensively and defensively at a variety of distances. It can be used effectively to attack the head or torso, as well as the arms and legs, and can set up attacking combinations by destroying the *kamae* or disrupting the balance of an opponent. Additionally, it has the unique ability to block both punches and kicks.

Begin by swinging your leg upward in a wide arc from the outside inward, with your knee slightly bent and the sole of your foot in a position of inversion. Continue executing in an arc, keeping your body upright, following through after you have made contact with your target. Great velocity is necessary to maximize the effectiveness of the kick.

Masterclass Karate

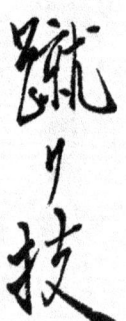

APPLICATION

In the following photos, the application of mikazuki geri is readily apparent, as it is shown here as a counterattack to jodan, chudan, and gedan levels.

Additionally, mikazuki geri can be used as mikazuki uke, to effectively block attacks from either the hands or the legs, or to destroy the posture or kamae of one's opponent.

MAWASHI UCHI (Inside Crescent Kick)

DESCRIPTION

Mawashi uchi is the inside version of the previously described mikazuki geri. It is therefore delivered in a similar manner, but comes from the outside to the inside with regard to the course of the kick, in an opposite direction from mikazuki geri. It generally uses the dorsal/lateral portion of the foot as the striking surface. It can be delivered to various targets at relatively close distances, and is difficult to defend against when executed properly.

Masterclass Karate

APPLICATION

The following sequence of photos shows various fighting applications of mawashi uchi.

Note that the applications show great similarity to those described in mikazuki geri.

Less Frequently Used Kicks

HIZA GERI (Knee Kick)

DESCRIPTION

Hiza geri is unique in that it is a powerful, devastating technique used primarily at close distances, nearly impossible to block. Utilizing the surface of the knee as the striking surface, it can be delivered along the same course as mae geri or mawashi geri, or can be directed in an upward or downward angle. Target areas include the groin, solar plexus, ribs, kidneys, and face. Particularly when used together in conjunction with the arms holding or pulling, hiza geri is a formidable part of the kicking arsenal.

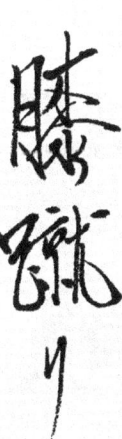

Masterclass Karate

APPLICATION

While at close range, the kick can be delivered in a variety of situations, and is seen in a number of the kata. The accompanying photos display various usages of hiza geri.

Attacking the head.

Attacking the ribs.

Attacking the groin.

Less Frequently Used Kicks

TOBI GERI (Jumping Kick)

DESCRIPTION

Tobi geri, though somewhat more limited in practical use, provides one with a formidable, powerful, sudden attack that is best executed from longer distances. Jumping allows the exponent to attack from a greater distance and adds the elements of height and surprise as the kick is being executed.

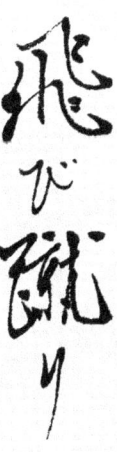

Conclusion

In the previous chapters I have described the kicks that are fundamentally essential to the understanding of karate-do. Without a complete understanding of these fundamental techniques, one cannot attain mastery of the art, nor can one get a glimpse of higher spiritual understanding. Mastery of kicking techniques will enhance all of the areas of your understanding of karate-do; your hand techniques will become better, your stances better, your balance and flexibility will improve, and metaphorically, you will become more stable, grounded, and free functioning.

Nothing can replace repetitive practice. Practice the techniques described with discipline, patience, and an open mind. Refine and polish consistently, again and again. Don't be satisfied. Question everything. Make your own discoveries. Make karate *your* karate.

I hope that this book has been a helpful introduction to your more complete development as a *budo-ka*, and to your further understanding of *"the way."*

Best of luck to you in your training…

Michael R. Berger

www.ingramcontent.com/pod-product-compliance
Lightning Source LLC
Chambersburg PA
CBHW081348080526
44588CB00016B/2409